Shugg's Pet Octopus

by Beverley Boorer

illustrated by Jan D'Silva

Harcourt Achieve

Rigby • Saxon • Steck-Vaughn

www.HarcourtAchieve.com
1.800.531.5015

Characters

Shugg

Sammy

Peter

Contents

Chapter 1

It Followed Me Home

Shugg dropped his tattered backpack on the floor. It was tattered because of Duke. Duke thought it was funny to throw Shugg's backpack around, and it always landed somewhere out of reach.

Like up on the basketball pole. Or on top of a six-foot fence — the sort with barbed wire on top. Shugg had not worked out how to solve this problem yet.

Shugg was not thinking about his problem
with Duke just now. He was thinking about the
octopus. Who would want an octopus for a pet?
No one. Not even Shugg. But somehow he had
one. It had followed him home from the beach,
and now it was sliding in through the cat door.

The cat hissed in fright and jumped up onto the bookcase. The dog yelped and hid behind the sofa. The parrot in the cage screeched, "Who's a pretty boy?" ten times.

Mom called from the computer room, "What's wrong with Tootoo, Shugg?"

"He doesn't like the octopus!" Shugg called back.

"That's not octopus in the fridge. It's calamari, and I told you not to feed Tootoo calamari rings!" Mom yelled.

Shugg looked at the octopus. One of its arms stirred the cat food. Another arm splashed into the dog's water bowl. A third arm pulled an open bag of chips off the table. "Calamari's a good name for you. Cal for short," said Shugg.

"Why are your socks in the bath?" she asked. "They should be in the washing machine."

"Don't touch them!" Shugg yelled. "I'll do it!"

While Shugg was getting dressed, his sister, Sammy, came into the bathroom. "Eeoowww!" she yelled. "Mom! Shugg's growing giant worms in the bath!"

"Don't worry about it," Mom called from the kitchen. "He's going to put them in the washing machine."

"Why would you put worms in the washing machine?" Sammy muttered. "This place is crazy."

Shugg pulled the plug out of the bath. "Come on, Cal. Here, boy," he whistled. By the time Shugg reached his room, the octopus was right behind him.

Shugg's brother, Peter, was on the top bunk reading a comic book. "Mom said we're not allowed to have another dog," Peter said without looking up.

Shugg dropped his backpack over Cal and pushed him under the bunkbed.

"So? I don't have a dog."

"We're not allowed to have snakes either."

"Who's got a snake? You've been reading too many comics!"

"Hey, Pete. What do octopuses eat?"

"Crabs and stuff, I think," Peter said as he jumped down from the top bunk and headed for the door. "Why?"

"No reason."

Peter looked down at the backpack poking out from under the bed. Then he shook his head. "Nah! Not even you would bring home an octopus."

Later that night, Shugg raided the pantry. He found a can of crabmeat and some lobster-flavored noodles. He opened both and pushed them under the bed.

Chapter 3

What's in the Bag?

The next morning, Shugg slept in. He quickly shoved his sandwiches into his backpack and ran out the door. His backpack felt heavy as he pounded along the pavement. He dragged it along the floor as he ran down the corridor to his classroom. He dropped it beside his desk and slid into his seat. Just in time.

Miss Stinger stopped by Shugg's desk. "Pick up that rubbish, Shugg," she said.

Shugg looked down. There was an empty noodle bag next to his feet. A rustling noise came from the backpack. Shugg stuffed the rubbish into his pocket and pushed the backpack further under his desk.

At lunchtime Shugg took his backpack to the fountain. He squirted water into it. Then he remembered his sandwich. The paper bag was soggy. It was also empty.

"You weren't supposed to eat my lunch," he said into the backpack.

"What's in your backpack, Shugg?" Katie asked.

"It's Cal, my octopus," Shugg said with a smile.

"Yeah," said Katie. "Right."

Duke folded his arms across his chest. "You got some lunch in that bag? Gimme it!" He snatched the backpack and pushed his hand into it. A strange look came over his face. "This feels like a . . . "

He tried to pull his hand out. "It feels like a
. . . " Duke flapped his hand and the backpack
around in the air. "It's a boa constrictor!"

The backpack flew off his hand. It sailed up in
the air. It landed right in Miss Stinger's lap.
Shugg ran up to Miss Stinger. "I'm sorry. It was
an accident."

Miss Stinger picked the backpack up between her index finger and her thumb. "This bag smells very . . . fishy. I don't think you should eat whatever is in there."

"Oh, no," said Shugg, "I won't."

"Go and buy some lunch," Miss Stinger said.
"And when you go home, wash out that bag."

"Yes, Miss Stinger, I will," said Shugg.

Chapter 4

Payback for Duke

Later, as Shugg and Katie walked home through the park, Duke stepped out from behind a tree. "Trying to scare me, were you?"

"No," said Shugg.

Duke snatched Shugg's backpack and threw it up into a very tall tree. He stood under the tree with his hands on his hips. "Now let's see you climb up and get it."

Shugg looked up into the tree. The backpack was caught on a limb. It was upside down. Cal was slowly sliding out.

"I don't think you should stand there," said Shugg. "Something might fall on you."

"Ha!" said Duke. "You can't fool me."

Cal dropped from branch to branch, down the tree. Katie began to giggle. Cal dropped off the last branch onto Duke's head. Two of Cal's arms held onto Duke's ears. Two of Cal's arms held onto Duke's hair. Two of Cal's arms held onto Duke's nose and chin. And two more of Cal's arms curled around Duke's neck.

"Aaaggghhh!!!" yelled Duke. He ran around in circles. He bumped into the tree. He bumped into the trash can. He almost bumped into Shugg and Katie. Then he fell into the pond.

Cal slid off his head and disappeared under the water. Duke crawled out of the water and disappeared into the bushes. Shugg climbed up the tree and grabbed his backpack.

Katie said, "This pond isn't even salt water."

"Cal doesn't mind," replied Shugg. Then he whistled, "Here, boy!"

Cal slid out of the water and into the backpack.

"A pet octopus," Katie said, shaking her head. "I've never heard of that."

Shugg grinned and slipped his backpack over his shoulders. "I don't think Duke will try and take my bag again," he said.

Glossary

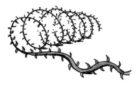
barbed wire
wire with sharp points that stick out

boa constrictor
a large snake that crushes its prey

calamari
squid that we eat as food

corridor
a long hallway with classrooms on either side

index finger
the first finger which is next to the thumb

limb
a large tree branch

octopus
a sea creature with eight long tentacles

raided
stole from

rustling
making a soft sound when moving

tattered
torn, ragged

Beverley Boorer

I saw a documentary on TV about someone doing an experiment. Crabs were kept in one tank and an octopus in another tank, on separate tables.

Each night the crabs would disappear. The staff hotly denied taking them home to eat. Finally, a hidden camera was set up.

It showed that the octopus would slide out of its tank, cross the floor to the crab's tank, where it had a midnight snack before returning home.

I thought, "Octopuses are so brainy, I must write a story about one!"

Jan D'Silva